CPSIA information can be obtained
at www.ICGtesting.com
Printed in the USA
LVHW062048231121
704221LV00030B/172

9 781087 807096